Eyes Like Pigeons
Roberta Rees

Brick Books

CANADIAN CATALOGUING IN PUBLICATION DATA

Rees, Roberta
  Eyes like pigeons

Poems.
ISBN 0-919626-61-0

I. Title.

PS8585.E44E9 1992   C811'.54   C93-093022-3
PR9199.3.R44E9 1992

The support of The Canada Council and the Ontario Arts
Council is gratefully acknowledged.

The cover is after an oil pastel drawing by Yvonne Markotic
entitled *Women Looking Down*.

Photos for sections I, II, III, VI, VIII and final photo
by M. J. Whalley. Photo for section V by Debbie Flynn.

Portions of this work have appeared or will appear in *Open Letter*.

Typeset in Ehrhardt, printed and bound by The Porcupine's
Quill. The stock is acid-free Zephyr Antique laid.

Brick Books
Box 38, Station B
London, Ontario
N6A 4V3

For Evelyn J., Thi H., and Kaloka

Means Poetry

Always back to this, Thi means poetry in Vietnamese, but what means meaning. Looking for the beginning, what means beginning. Six seven eight years ago, looking through the windows streaked classroom windows out out everybody look out. Big blue dumpster condoms in a concrete alley fan of a cheap steak place smoking Wendy's plastic in the sun. Jerry in black leather jacket long hair pale eyes, older brother shot himself in the bedroom upstairs, shit was I scared to go up there man shit, but I had to, see, 'cause he was next older than me and shit I couldn't let Marvin see he can't handle things Marvin. Looks out the window, tips his chair back, croons, Any of you ever touch Miss Rees or ever say an unsavory word man and I'll break your fuckin' heads. Marcia in the back black-lined eyes, coal kohl Lady Mabelline lifted from Woolco across the parking lot surrounded by concrete. Look Miss Rees don't tell no one but my brother-in-law touches me again and I'll rip his face off, bottom lip curved naked pink sun streaking the window big blue dumpster Wendy fuckin'g grinning on the plastic sign across the street, trembles. In grade ten Laura stares and stares at me, green green eyes green as my mother's, talks about running her horse, big Thoroughbred full speed in the ditch along the road to Bragg Creek, hangs around my desk, Listen you wanna come riding Saturday, staring, her eyes green, and my mother's eyes green running from the police at twelve, her mother lost in the graveyard God knows where. Hangs around my desk, Laura, late sun sinking behind Wendy's behind Woolco behind Ponderosa Steak House behind wires and wires up the hill behind the police station. Sits in a chair so close her eyes jiggle, jiggles her feet bites her lip, I think I figured something out, eyes fierce green and hair fine like my mother's, I been thinking and I figured it out, I'm adopted and I figured out you're my mom.

Was this when   Thi
          means poetry   you
  what   twelve   thirteen?   When
          you still ate   when
                round face grinning
    short hair   round arms   ripe armpits
and sun streaking what grey green orange the window pane?

The word desire has nothing to do with beat beat beat in the groin, pulse pulse behind the eyes. Surge of heat in the fingertips makes you want to squeeze press bite. But the word desire, de sire. Nothing.

My brother worked for two years in Ponoka, the brother whose tiny blue-veined body smashed his bed against the wall convulsing and shuddering on hands and knees chest on fire trying to breathe the room filled with airless phantoms. They hallucinate, he says, some every ten seconds and who are we to say only one of the three people talking is real. They see Christ and God and the Holy Spirit Incarnate, but none of them ever sees Mary, not even the women. One man almost finished a ph.d. on Nietszche in Cambridge keeps drawing God. He keeps God under his pillow for a night or two but always gives him away because God's eyes burn his neck. My brother's favorite is schizophrenic and retarded. When he was a baby his father tied him to the bed and beat him. Now he pulls his toenails out in the night, pushes a pencil up his nose into his brain. My brother hugs him, Doesn't it hurt? Oh yes. He needs a constant companion, this man, he cannot be trusted not to kill himself or anyone else not to play in his own shit. He is 6'3", and his Constant takes away cigarettes, bubble gum, time playing with my brother in the pool, when he does something his Constant tells him is inappropriate. One day he says to my brother, Al, do you have kids? No, my brother says, why? Because I'd like to be your kid, that's why. He looks at his Constant, I know that's inappropriate, but I would. Then he asks my brother, Do you have a wife, Al? Yes, I do, she works here too. Oh, he nods at his Constant, I know this is not appropriate, but Al, I would like to be your wife, I would.

always
at the front of the class
hand in the air

Cathy you called yourself not Thi not poetry

schoolgirl comicbook   Cathy

round face the only brown always long answers out loud
English the others couldn't understand but beautiful about
Shakespeare blood flowers Wiebe's angel whatever and grinning

but your dictionary   Vietnamese

thin thin pages and between

your finger long thin stroking

❀

The year before Thi we had a party. Lined the desks in the middle of the room for food. Kamal brought sheets of pita, paper-thin, at least two feet in diameter his mother made that morning. And tabouli in a tub we ate all day. Selma brought curried mung beans and dahl and vegetable samosas. Demetri baklava and galaktombouroko, custard oozing from layers of filo. Raymond Mah brought tapes of Glenn Gould playing the Goldberg Variations and a book with Karsh's portrait of Gould at his grand piano. Tung and Tran brought a bakery cake in a box. Laughed when we opened the box. Sat on desktops and laughed until their heads touched their knees whenever anyone looked at, touched, or cut a piece of thick white cake with pink icing.

In the hallway Chau Bui runs up to me, please Miss Rees, I think you don't know me and this is a problem I think, I am asking you come to my house New Year, my father he ask you too. His eyes shift from mine to the floor. He ducks away down the hall. A sneaky character, another teacher says over my shoulder, don't trust him (in Vietnam, Thi tells me years later, you spend New Year's with your teacher. Everyone respects the teacher.)

Chau's mother and sisters and aunts and girl cousins line up in the kitchen, bow to Michael and me (across the city in my sister's house my father lies in a dark room, chemicals oozing out his pores, creeping up the back of his throat, and I want to hug these women with eyes like pigeons and bright coloured tunics but eyes like pigeons is a cliché in Vietnamese writing Thi tells me many years later when she stops erasing Vietnamese with her finger and that is another story except for my mother and sister in my sister's living room New Year's Eve reading Louis L'Amour and A Bird in the House every cell even the cells in the backs of their eyes listening for the gag then heave from the bedroom.)

We sit in the living room with Chau's father and uncles, talk French because we can't speak Vietnamese and they can't speak English. We eat soup, big pieces of meat and vegetable Chau's mother brings in from the kitchen. Chau's father sits on the edge of the couch, dark suit and his eyes dark, says he is happy to be here in Canada, happy his son will go to university, happy to use the language of his country's occupation, très très heureux (in the dark dying on his back chemicals burning the insides of his veins leak out leak over his tongue vapours like rubbing alcohol evaporating his spirit evaporating cold in the room and you can't catch vapours you can't hold ether hold his head burning hot on your neck you cannot stop him evaporating, then Thi the summer she lives with you reads Vietnamese late at night says she saw Chau at the Buddhist church his father died of cancer she didn't know how old maybe fifty fifty-one same as, but this is later except for the chopsticks and chunks of meat and the cold wind in my sister's bedroom.)

We go downstairs with Chau and his cousins. They turn music up up, until the wood-panelled walls shake. We dance wildly. The mothers and fathers sit above us.

in this city are   words   are sentences are
      conjunctions   looking for
              space   looking for
                time
    in this city are parents
               from other countries   from

in this city
    girls whose fathers pick them up at school who
        go to Greece marry a Greek boy who   in this city
   Kamal's father left   his mother her beautiful
beautiful boy   cooked and cleaned for
        Tran fifteen worked nights mother in Australia
father in Sweden   worked nights   sent money
   Allea's father slaps her she studies hard can't wait
marries a man from Lebanon   in this city
  Tong runs a paper was a soldier must
free his   in this   in this

    in

      in

     basement

     book

         girl

Vietnam

         city, here

Fine, Laura says, fine, you think you're too young to be my mom, fine, I thought maybe she was Irish or Welsh had eyes same colour as yours about the same height musta been real young, but fine, just fine. Green eyes narrow, black tights black shirt black cape black, turns the lights out, one two strikes a match thirteen candles in a circle on the floor reclines in the centre candlelight in the green my mother's eyes green as, red her lips fingernails in black flickering and to the others black flickering, this is Satan's circle Satan's in this room in the corners behind you look behind you look at me do I look like Satan do I look like Satan's bride, or mother, how about mother. Or slamming her books on her desk walking past mine head high turned away blonde hair fine as, her hand shaking shakes her head mutters under her breath, She musta been real young maybe fourteen maybe thirteen. Sits at the back green glaring all term, green glaring and Susan's eyes green but not the same not the same year, darker warmer, but her hair fine and clover-honey and in the photos my mother on a back-alley balcony, fire escapes wires wooden railings pedal pushers and what thirteen fourteen on her own because her mom was dead her sister Edna dead her father beat her when he drank shouted You shoulda died instead, kneels kisses the boy she is babysitting who is crying for his mummy, lips big and soft and thirteen fourteen, Susan by the window in the sun, wires and cement and stench from the dumpster, I'm gonna be a hooker have clothes money a steady job. Rhonda in the back light pink lipstick ironed creases in her pants flowered blouse, My mom didn't want me but my gramma raised me a Christian taught me right from wrong, see my ring I'm gonna marry him right away get pregnant right away.

Yet later a year or two it was you who phoned

    alone in the dark so soft so soft

your voice and Thi rhymes

        with tea with Cathy with poetry.

❖

& what if
you had walked down the hall
past my door
into someone else's class

what if you
what if &
running for the boat running
plums like earlobes you said
your mother running after you calling your
name &
just what if

& your sister
what about her what about
a refugee camp a refugee island
you said, come our brother said
come &
her lips like plums on a young man's throat by the sea
& you were angry what then &
after, when he sailed, what if we say sailed

A different country altogether

And so we have sailed and come, but your sister
up to her breasts in salt water, the young man sailing
away   &   a name from the ocean from the sea
draping her shoulders
like seaweed
like hair
the most beautiful, you said
eleven children, you said, one sister dead
six in Vietnam
you & two brothers & your sister combing her name
Helen goddamn it, so what if

the young man had not sailed away
had not married someone else
your dead sister had not
another sister's husband had not
poisoned the fetus curled shrimp in her gut
poisoning her,   what if

Shakespeare had a sister the alphabet were round
& it's been   what   seven years since
you my classroom your round face
lapping English
the air &

if

Not you but another, telling
whole class white but
her sister
a girl
Vietnamese
smiling

trucks big like this, she says, vvvvrrrmmmmmm, like this
vvvrrrmmmmm vvvvrrrmmmm, like this waiting outside a village
her village her sisters, like this
full of women, like this

the truck waited
revving
diesel
soldiers guns dust &
a man ran &
threw his baby like this (she is smiling) into the air his wife in
the truck unfurling her arms &

If you hold your breath long enough you can hear the sea in
every cell lapping each cell wall, & if thirty people hold their
breaths together listening to the silence in a room after the
voice recedes, salt stings the moon & you can hardly tell water
from water

Or context. Which year, what names, what chemistry colours shapes bodies hands eyes mothers fathers sisters brothers tastes and smells. Robin at the front eyes pale blue shaking and rolling and her fingers and magnifying glass finding the letters pinning the alphabet, I'm legally blind but I can see shapes like down a tunnel, if I put them together I can think words do all the work on my own write my own essays look how neat, fingers long and cool. And blue, sits by my desk, see how blue my fingernails and cold I wondered why I was so cold and tired my mother took me to her doctor says I have leukemia start chemotherapy next week but I won't miss class and don't tell my brother, he's sensitive our father died grade twelve is important, my mother and I aren't telling him either. Kieu in the front seat by the door, hair bobbed a white blouse short black skirt tapered fingers head down ankles crossed dictionary against her wrist writes about crossing the South China Sea, how the boat was crowded and hot and the engine stopped the wind wouldn't blow, how the woman rocked her baby stopped crying rocked and rocked her an older woman took her from her arms rolled the baby over the side and they caught seagulls with string but they starved one after another rolled over into the sea and the sun and no wind no food no toilet no mother no father but her cousin she loved the last two alive no drinking water no food closed his eyes and died and she was the only one alone on the boat and the sea the sun the boat with the motor pulling up beside. Mo in her big body onstage, not playing but being, being anyone in another body, introduces her mom and dad she looks just like, gets roles in school, sure, but tougher in university in a big body, but better than the pretties better than the players, becomes just becomes even her body, gives up acting. My mom, too, after her mother died after her sister died after the kids calling her More Ass and Tits than Anything Else after the teacher saying Your sneakers stink after her father in their shack beat her, wanted to act she could taste it, grade eight left her books on her desk walked out, They don't stink. My mother washed them I do too.

```
                              stories. face of a child.
they all write their              Kieu writes. her.
writing writing their             fingers. desk. chalk.
ordinary
summer vacation stories
incest stories leukemia stories love and
                                    zit. bra.
from
                              Canada but whose. basketball
maybe


                              or dance in the gym. pen.
their fingers ears bones
                        pencil. light switch. walkman.
hanging, hanging onto
                              book. boyfriend. story.
her round face and frown
                              Kieu. her.
tell don't tell tell don't tell
                              air-conditioner.
be one fit in be one fit
                                    Kieu.
Vietnam her head her story
                        socks skirt t-shirt running shoes
story her head in
                              Kieu Kieu Ki
```

blackboard eraser reader ink jeans intercom text teen-ager story
ordinary ordinary ordinary ordinary ordinary ordinary ordinary

When South China Sea

When the sun careless in the middle of the sky

When gulls flapping and crying

When flesh from bones

When babies' voices in their throats

When skin

When rolled over the side of the boat

When string & the raw flesh of gulls

When Kieu's lover

When the gull staring & staring

When her lover's lips

When his dead body

When her teeth

When the gull

When the far down deep splashing

The heron unfurling its neck like a question mark reaching claws
& legs long into the sea, its wings & like an old sea-salt
horking

Eyes Like Pigeons

❁

i am thinking silence
silently about silence
Watch my mouth

Dreaming a dream
Two baby girls encased in
beef, raw purple beef
see the grain of meat
the grain of their baby cheeks
deep in beef
rock them encased
one in a thick slab like roast
the other in a steak
rock them in my bare
meat against my arms, surely you see
& a black yearling heifer butts my
pushes her flat black head into my
Stay off the couch i sing &

The problem
The English accent, in Jamaica, if you
please please do not, girls, do not
leave the door open when your father is
not home, now this poor girl
everynight must sleep under, yes
, under the porch,
              only one thin blanket because she opened
              the door when her father was not home
              please girls, you must please, girls, please
              your fathers & brothers & now
              if anyone wants to buy this baby,
              born just this April past, call

i am listening to the silence in my abdomen
my mouth in the mirror
watch

Fourteen floors above fourteenth street
fourteen years old or fifteen or sixteen
In the countryside in Vietnam they don't count
birth days

Count them, how many
in Canada
in Calgary, how many
count

Listen to Thi's silence in the corner
music Vietnamese the ghetto blaster planted
meat simmering a shiny aluminum pot &
pictures mother father sisters & Helen planted
& the books can't forget
English, sun slicing their pages planted
an alphabet
Listen to her silence, read the walls table, the pot
on the stove the books, her mother's face, hair pulled
back, plants & plants

reads Vietnamese briefly, her finger conducting

This alphabet
This poem
This silence hearing and dreaming in my abdomen
Thi for her mother
& her mother's head hair all the way to floor
aches

the story she writes
her mother's hair
rooted in Vietnamese soil
reading

her mouth

❀

Whose history whose voice whose boat whose
force 8 sea 50 knot winds 15 foot waves
overcast   no celestial
navigation (doldrums
                in the South China Sea
    and one baby)
50,000 tons eight 15 foot guns capable of
firing 1 ton shells 24 miles (junk rigging
                on these small boats
                    no boom just a single sail
        luff ing in
                    the hot not wind)
Freak hit torpedo launched by vintage WWI
biplane   knocked out steering   10 am. May 27 1941 captain
ordered crew to open seacocks   maiden voyage
                    maiden Titanic
                    Bismarck
            (boat people)
10:30 am. hit by 3 torpedoes from British cruiser Dorsetshire
sank 3 minutes later several hundred swimming
when the ship went down   Uncle George
                    not my uncle my husband's
                on deck the Tartar   smokes a soggy
                    cigarette watches the Bismarck
        sink   writes a poem
                (the baby does not cry or blink
                        on the South China Sea)
800 in the water the Dorsetshire picked up 100 thought
they saw a periscope left 700 to drown (South China Sea
                say it
        South China Sea   starving
                    not drowning   rolled
                            over)

1912 the Titanic sank 12,000 feet of water. 1,500 drowned. Dr.
Robert Ballard discovered shoes and boots all over the ocean
floor animals won't eat processed leather, they eat the body and
clothes but they won't eat leather   (bare feet and
                                                    eyes like pigeons

Or the body, say. Which one we inhabit and how. And where, where in the warm tissues, membranes, arteries, cilia waving rocking brushing, i want to say sea-grass, the ocean big and breathing. How and where and if. And how we stop eating our eyes grow bigger and bigger. In a mall in China Town, a Vietnamese fast-food, cold sweet coffee green jelly rice cake, a young woman walks by, long hair round eyes, thin thin. Thi grabs my arm, That's the ideal beauty for Vietnamese women, eyes like pigeons. Stops eating. Too big for Vietnamese too muscular eyes too narrow, hate my body Roberta, you must understand. Eyes like, looks in the mirror, walks in all the bathrooms looks in all the mirrors. Pigeons. In classical Vietnamese writing. A cliché, she says. More submissive, she says, I must be more submissive. Women with eyes like pigeons. Pigeons. Billboards, movies, books, paintings. I. Body. Hate. Eyes like. Thighs arms bums cheeks skin, thinner and thinner and thinner. Two sips of broth, leaves noodles pork shrimp in her bowl. Rips a piece of napkin, rolls and rolls between thumb and finger. Thinner and thinner. Voice. Thinner and thinner. Whisper: too muscular too round too solid too Canadian too Oriental too selfish, tooo toooooo tooooooooo. Or not enough. Not quiet enough obedient enough sociable enough smart enough light enough dark enough. Eyes like. In Vietnam not enough food. In the camps on Pulau Bidong, on the boats, never enough food. Eyes like. 17 18 19, on my back in a basement apartment. Like pigeons. On my back. Stomach, hip-bones, pelvic bones, eye sockets. On my own, starving memory from my cells, starving memory of. Pain in. Memory of. In. An apple even, teeth the skin juice tongue throat. Chocolate uvula smooth wet oh scent tongue tip of soft yes soft palette. Look, don't touch. Eyes like. Too. Not enough. Too. Not enough. Too too too. Not not not. Starving sssshhhhh look at sssshhhhh don't sssshhhhh. Mushroom. Pear. Butter. Corn syrup. Look. Be looked at. But don't touch. Almond. Caramel. Custard. Look. Cream. Look. Strawberry. Look. Don't. Marzipan. Don't. Shrimp. Don't. Tacos tortilla sour cream. Don't don't don't. When i faint, when a rash covers my body, when i can't write my finals, when i cook for my room-mate my family weigh each kernel of corn each carrot stick, when my heart flutters my period stops for two years, when my reflection disappears in the mirror, my throat will not say i. Buck up, the doctor says, chucks my knee, you're being silly. Mad, i write on scraps of paper to the professor, Abnormal Psychology, i am going mad dream and dream about food over and over and over rehearse over and over walking sleeping in class on the couch over and over mad can't eat people starving their eyes this body hate drink ten glasses of water weigh each pea dream hamburger spring rolls stilton cheese an olive must not my eyes must not breasts thighs bum stomach must not mad don't think talk remember tongue teeth a cherry doughnut liver pickle pie prime rib drumstick pimento just not over and over ketchup lard ham potato must not must not. One bite, chocolate, i have sinned, weak, sinned, cram four chocolate bars two bags of chips, sinned, twenty-four red licorice loaf of bread with cottage cheese and corn syrup stuff i hate stuff my mouth hate my throat eyes my hate two cakes half a pie a dozen cookies cram hate bag of marshmallows dizzy hate eyes like hate gallon of ice cream hate can't think hate can't remember hate can't dizzy hate hate hate. Hide my notes in the back of my book, slip out the back door. Dizzy. Eyes down, swollen. Into the bathroom. Look in all the mirrors. Stupid, the girl in all the mirrors, stupid. Go away, leave me alone, go away, fuck off. Eyes swollen. Sits on the toilet, her head in my hand, swollen bloated pain in her gut nauseous. No one loves you, i say. Move my hand. Her forehead falls onto her bare thighs. Bitch, stupid bitch. My sister, too, eyes like, staring at all the food. Nibbles watermelon, pushes it away, I'm stuffed. Hips. Calves. Breasts. Smaller and smaller. Eyes like. A man at a party leans over speaks to her breasts, Did anyone ever tell you you have beautiful mammaries. Can I touch one. Walks away, voice loud, Don't be such a bitch, better learn to take a compliment, touchy bitch. Her cheekbones, veins in her temples, eyes round and vacant and staring and the summer she goes to Oregon with our parents, nibbles on a watermelon, pushes it away. Goes to the bathroom. Stops in all the towns, Have to get something at the drugstore. Our mom follows her around, finds her picking up two boxes of Ex-lax, our dad in the car sweating cold sweat, dying, no one has said yet, holds a peach to his lips, heaves, drops his head back eyes closed, so tired so goddamn tired. Fat boy, that fat boy smells, but thin when she met him, a jockey, only left-overs, hours in the sweat-box, Bennies, and the horses, god the horses. Thin, she was always thin, More Ass and Tits than anything else the boys called, lard on bread and a garden before her mother died, lots of cabbage. Chunks of chocolate from the men unloading the box-car, Shit, broke another one, here kid you better take it. Sold to buy medicine for her mom on hands and knees wheezing choking. More Ass and Tits, and the man a stranger dragging her by the railway tracks, I wanna fuck Shirley Temple I wanna sink my teeth into Shirley Temple's ass I wanna make Shirley Temple bleed dammit. French fries, pork fat, raw hamburger, lard. By the sink turned away. Eyes like. At the table hardly eats, pushes her plate away, my sister too. Fatter and fatter. Hate, hate. My dad a butcher a singer fat-boy cells remembering, stuffs bologna head-cheese weiners Capicola Mortadella garlic sausage in his mouth his cheeks, stuffs and stuffs. My mom catches him with another woman a singer tall slim. Starves herself three months hardly a bite looks like her mother cheeks sunken eyes black. He stops singing moves back home stops going out, stops. On the couch bloated another peanut butter cookie half an apple-pie chocolate cake, How can you forgive me. In the kitchen, Jim's Café uptown, she swallows chips and gravy, hamburger and gravy, beef and gravy, puffs a Players Plain. Memory in her cells, eyes like. And when she stays over in the summer, Thi means poetry, poetry, we eat sesame-squares fig-bars, tofu and noodles, says Eating almost feels normal. In the university library, tenth floor, a man wearing sunglasses sits beside her, pulls himself off. On the phone, the green chair in the living room, Did you report him? No, I went and looked in the bathroom mirror. On the ceiling, my mom tells, i was on the ceiling watching myself. Eyes like. My sister steps out of the shower, Tell me honestly, are my breasts repulsive? A Buddhist nun, Thi tells me, with her long arms, eyes like, beside the river, a bean paste cake a pineapple bun. Invites me to Vietnamese New Year, hundreds of people, translates the Buddhist teacher's words over the microphone. Her father she hasn't seen for years sits on the end of her bed, laughing telling he will marry her off and she translates. I can't respect you her older brother says, too Canadian, lives with his family speaks Vietnamese her nieces and nephews English. Pineapple bun, her long fingers. Have a piece, she says, eat. And her eyes.

❀

                    why
        eyes like pigeons
            i in pigeons   birds
                pluck the eyes
            the eyes of
                        woe
                pluck   the   e
                women
                        in classical   Viet
            namese
                        stories
why   cooo   cooo   cooo   o
                woe   o   woe   o
        pluck   the   e   womn
                pluck the i   pluck the i   pluck the
                        i

❀

rock the sea
beneath the boat
see and an s
between i and land
before he so
she lands they
on an island
no m before mother
mmmmmmmmmmmmmmmm
other so   b and r
brother with an s
listen for the space
between th   and   i
listen for the s
sssssssssssssssss
ister   and i
land in the sea
say Puuuu-lau
Beeee-dong
say i see   s
ssssss-ister
stroke a young man's lips

stroke l   stroke s
breathe hhhhh–ip
s before ail they
brothers and sisters
cross the sea
the man sails south
could be mouth
mmmmmmmmmmmmmmmmmmmmmm
outh her sister
north   now strike
u out of guilt
or i try i
gilt or gulls
on South China Sea
write cry

Red Bean Paste Cakes & Jelly Grass

❖

in Vietnamese means poetry Thi but what means meaning
dancing in her brother's basement body and hair
her mother in Vietnam brushes hair to floor
Thi here brushing hair walls ceiling always books sings
sings her head inside sweating her body basement
dancing midnight and there she says you are my
mother brushes her hair into dirt floor
you are small like her my feet too big but
running the boat her brother plums from the trees
away red and white black her mother's hair to floor
running her name Thi Thi Thi mother's head aching
always never too late her hands in Thi's head brushing
her brother on the boat too many mouths shouting
ma on the shore mouths words and
alone books her body flinging her head dancing

In the living room, in the green chair
In the living room in the green chair or over the phone in the dark
In the living room the green chair the dark in any case your voice
More likely Prince's Island, rain and the river divided
Rain in the leaves
Cottonwood leaves dropping rain on our shoulders
Prince's Island with the rain and the river
Divided
Red bean paste buns
Red bean paste cakes
Red bean paste cakes with a yolk in the middle
Jelly lemon grass, the books you pull out of your bag
Always books, and the nights you stay over
The weeks in the summer you sleep over
Staying up late reading Vietnamese at last
Getting up sitting in the living room in the green chair in the
dark, reading

The green chair in the living room always there
And the living room because of the word 'living'
Your words missing, because i am afraid to influence
Because i am afraid of influence
confluence
Prince's Island just upriver from the confluence of the Bow and
Elbow
Just west of China Town where we buy red bean paste buns
Where we buy red bean paste cakes with dry yolks, and cans of
jelly grass

✺

One of the popular boys picks me up in a purple car, don't know
why me except maybe his girlfriend told him to fuck off, just fuck
right off, probably for drinking. Picks me up in a purple Pontiac
smells like Irish Spring and hockey pads and rye whisky. Hands
me a brown chicken clucking, Could you hold Louise, she wants
to come to this party, can't leave Louise home, somebody might
eat her, hey Louise, hey chick-chick-chick. Holding Louise,
heartbeat my thigh, buck-buck-buck her throat my fingers,
feathers my crotch, warm oh warm. He shoves the car into Drive,
floors it. Through Bellevue, the Frank Slide, Blairmore, Coleman,
up the Forestry Trunk Road, the hair black curled on his neck
warm skin soap booze air freshener and Louise, Louise. And i
can't think of a thing to say, don't know what i'm doing here
holding his chicken except his fingers hard and brown from
working the mine, me one year away in the city back for summer
and my crotch, my crotch. Fish-tailing up the Forestry Road and
the pines, mmmmmmmmm the pines, not talking touching
nothing. I carry Louise into the cabin on my arm, pulse and warm
skin and feathers, put her up on a rafter, Be safe, Louise, be safe.
He talks with his friends, laughs and talks and turns his face so he
can look sideways at his girlfriend talking and laughing with her
friends, drinks and drinks. I stand by the door invisible, cool air
mountains black jagged pines the pulse in my groin Louise up in
the rafter throat song. He holds his glass up to Louise, his friends
hold their glasses up, beer whisky gin, she dip dip dips. All the
cheekbones, eyes blue green brown lavender indigo chartreuse dun
chestnut hazel, fingers scooped tapered pillowed flat thick bony
spread hooked fisted, rye on their breath gin on their breath, beer
baby duck cherry liqueur, voices in their throats, and i want to go
home with them all of them talk to their mothers and fathers, tell
me what your bodies remember how you sleep what you eat how
you breathe in Keilbossa cottage cheese gnocchi vereniki halubsha
gripe water toilet water tobacco and the smells of your sleeping
what you see when you close your eyes. Her lids drop and she
sways on the rafter forward back forward, groans, falls. Scrabbles

43

in circles on the floor, clucks and moans and white mucous drips from her beak. They stand around her laughing, Look at the goddamn chicken she's goddamn drunk. When I pick her up, Hey, Leave her there, she's havin' a good time, hold her shaking to my chest, You're okay you'll be okay Louise Louise chick-chick-chick. Drops me off the sun coming up over the mountains, the purple Pontiac vibrates in front of our house, Louise passed out on my knee, See ya. Hardly looks at me, purple Pontiac in the sun, humming in the sun, away. Or in a white Buick, parked on the old Frank Road, limestone boulders black against the sky, Turtle Mountain black against the sky and Frank Lake breathing cold, so pissed his eyes flutter, lays his head on my chest, You're too good for me she won't even talk to said she still loves me what are you doing with, Jesus Jesus Jesus. And in Calgary in the dark on the floor his hand stroking my face his voice in the dark on my cheek, She'll come back I know she will just has to try it out he's a med. student she needs that I can wait two more years before I graduate I can wait. Smells like limes. Pulse in my groin ache in my groin his hand on my forehead cheek eyelids temple that's all. Twenty-one a drug dealer out of prison let me show you baby had to think love not desire not lust not i want to pull you inside flex my muscles young and wet and strong.

you listen, Roberta, but you never tell me about yourself

44

✿

multiculturalism is ruining this country said my friend we should
all just be Canadian come here and be One Happy Family and in
the village where I grew up Bellevue 1700 people and 35
nationalities and in our own home one Man one Woman two Girls
two Boys and one Black Dog Bootsie Spitz hunting dog but a runt
never grew ran down rabbits bigger than him took on an Alaskan
Malamute lost his eye almost his leg stitched back on imagined
himself a Big Body all the dogs in Bellevue just like him in his Big
Body and my sister remembers the weight of her chest her aching
shoulders and eyes dirty dirty slut slut watching her breasts never
her face invasion of eyes like hands like feet like all those pricks
speaking for her breasts wishes she could be a ventriloquist have
her breasts say hey what the fuck you looking at buddy keep your
eyes on your own body your own Canada my father said he'd send
me to Australia more hormones in beef there maybe you'll grow
breasts and my brothers one fair asthmatic scrawny the other dark
played hockey and not just Bellevue but in our home my sister
sewed cleaned cooked a pact with Mom Carol can say anything to
but i was the oldest rode horses built fences shot a rifle at five
always with men privy their talk until breasts and rules changed
sure just small breasts but female hid it all wore five pairs of
underpants washed them at night raged at my mom and my sister
this summer said a boy we all knew raped her behind the arena
never told thought she deserved while one brother inside shooting
pucks slap-shots all his friends his father the coach the other
outside gasping in a snowbank until someone found him rushed
him to hospital alone in an oxygen tent our mom was raped too
when she was eleven same year her mom died of asthma heart
exploded her father drank beat her this was in Calgary where my
friend grew up my mom ran to a stranger's stood on the step i
need my mom my friend married an older man cooks cleans and
referees him and their two grown sons one in university the other
pissed at the world she starves grows fatter and fatter almost died
this fall a colostomy speaks her husband's words her father a
minister my mother's father a drunk my brother's friend from

Yugoslavia three days on trial accused of stealing a test box he
built his former employer sued said I brought Zrinko over now
look no gratitude police said don't your mom and dad teach you
not to steal over there now you come here fuckin' thief and Iqbal
from Kuwait pockets the purple starfish sand-dollar sea-urchin
my mom shows him thank you thank you a year later phones
thank you for the gifts who the hell oh Iqbal who stole your
accent Thi and i talking where she worked out front near the
counter the manager comes up says to me can I help you welcome
to Canada says Iqbal and Thi and Zrinko and Bootsie with his one
eye   sewn-on leg   Big Imagined Body.

Where the Blue Is

❃

Always back to this, Thi means poetry in Vietnamese, but what means meaning. Or beginning. Mother, Mom, Mummy, Evelyn, Evvie, Eve. I hate Eve, she says, it's a disgusting name, call me Ev or Evvie, but forget Eve. Stands on a chair, sings into the lightbulb, I saw the li-i-ight, I saw the li-i-ight. On her own at thirteen, running, running from. Says on the phone, My uncle wouldn't take me and Gord after Mom died, said he didn't want no little bastard kids. Sixteen, watches a boy maybe eighteen walk into the Stampede Bar and Grill, greasy burgers chips coffee and smells so damn good in the morning feels so damn good the Hi Evvies the How ya doing Evvies the No one makes coffee like you Evvie, Lookin' good, kid, lookin' real good. Watches him walk in dark and fine-boned with her friend Garth, Like you to meet Bobby here, a jockey on the track. Watches him close his eyes kiss the woman married and older and her voice husky husky, Come down to the store darlin' got something to show you, watches them whisper in the record store, disappear together into a sound room, close the door. Outside when they sing at her mother's funeral. Outside when they sing. Watches him outside the Stampede Bar and Grill standing under a tree, her inside, hamburgers fries coffee pie, money in her pocket, heart in her chest, watches him out under the tree watching her, inside out, money in her pocket, New Year's tickets from her boss in her pocket, steam and mustard and relish and You're a good girl Evvie, you're a good girl, How about another coffee here, Evvie. Walks out to him under the tree, snow in his hair, booze and, She dumped me Evvie. Climbs in his window, no girls allowed, climbs into his room his bed. Holds him, It's okay you're good you're smart you'll be okay.

even if her mother from the dead
         or yours   even   then
lost
    all those years nights alone longing years and years
                           child

❀

Thi reads in the library everyday tenth floor english
Atwood Woolf Ondaatje her finger
    caresses words lifts off pages licks her finger dances
back arched vowels loving the dark
    her arms the alphabet lips black black he is in the library how
how old are you lonely lonely running in the running
    rwuanda everyday rifles bones bodies sshhhh ssshhhhh her lips
how how old twice as ssshhhhh ssshhhhh her fingers lips
    here and here dark in the spreading here and thighs vowels
open his lips thighs too old I am sssshhhhh her mouth
    breath breast vulva black in vowel tongue roll
want

✿

or the body   say

which one we in   habit   in

side   i   my   body   i

in oh in warm tissues membranes arteries cilia

                                        wave   rock   brush

i   in   ing

want   i want   tongue   mine i   eye   say

          sea-grass   ocean   my   me

               big and breathe

     in   in   in   in

side   wide   my

          whose and how and where and if

                              ffffffffffff

❀

Carol

my sister not a Christmas Carol cheeks like an Inuit i was
three called her Kaloka inherited the Welsh voice with a vibrato a
bell all chromatically tuned carillon sounds too much like carrion
she loved to eat bugs plonked on the lawn there's a picture see
Carol on the grass cheeks like an Inuit beside the house where we
lived four of us downstairs from Detluff and his mom and dad
ours worked at Burns blood and singed on the pig killing floor ran
knives up the pig's asses dropped them in boiling water some still
alive squealing and trying to climb out he puked couldn't work
there worked cutting sides of beef already skinned boss ordered
him kill one of the steers he held the gun to her head supposed to
stun her cut her throat couldn't pull the trigger she charged him
up the board fence grabbed his shoulder she wasn't really a she
but that's Carol on the lawn chasing bugs with her worming finger
forehead wrinkled concentrating a spider high stepping we sleep
together later in Bellevue wind shaking shaking our house our
dark bedroom huddled sloped ceiling we can touch Carol draws
on my back turned to her don't look only once rub her back sick
to her stomach flu my mom says Carol tells me later she was
stoned speed or lsd walked home one foot in the ditch all the way
home down the long hill wind whistling inside her head hugging
her breasts she hated hated they came one summer pushed out
her bathing suit spilled over top slut said the boys in school she
grew her hair long walked on the hems of her jeans narrowed her
eyes blank slut her friend's father called her in the Bellevue arena
ours slammed him into the boards don't you ever speak to my
daughter that way you asshole ripped her jeans at the knees why
do you slouch around her breasts arms   stiff   Carol
Lynn   carillon   couldn't stop hugging   her   cheeks like an
Inuit

Kaloka

✿

Kaloka Pagoda in a blue blue photo

Thailand Sighland can't say my land
                              but wish i knew
                                  wish i flew
            sixteen years of breasts getting me down
            get down low down won't take my coat off
amazing how yours were like raisins/

            sister sister walk me across the floor
            you afraid?
            afraid afraid all those eyes

    me Kaloka in the photo i
              i sigh fly
            i in Indonesia
        twelve twelve years ago under anaesthesia

    are they ugly
    am i ugly
    look at
    don't look at
    do you love me   /but listen
                                          sister
remember what that plastic surgeon
remember what he said that plastic day
    you lie here my little one/ and you lie here my honey bun
    a little snip a little slice/ a little give a little take

53

but when the needle
when his hands
when masks and gowns
when orange ink
when circles around
when the knife
when my nipples
only i
i me Kaloka
hold my hand
hold my
hand my
hold
hold

aaaahhhh
but speaking Thai in the long gow sun
breasts my arms thighs my brown
tongue tongue tongue
yes oh yes curling unfurling yes
on my cheek against my eye
turgid twisting listen ain't resistin'
snake across my face

slut. is what the boys. and grown men let me let me let me.
fuckin' babies. bat the nipple when she don't let down. your fault bitch.
you make me want. and lips and teeth. let me. give me. I want. and
rock at night sharpen nails hook under all this goddamned weight this
goddamned flesh these goddamned goddamned goddamned they are not
me there is no room for i.

                    thigh sigh thai
                    nipple ripple cripple

          the man smiling says
                    this is what you're born with
     baby   luck of the draw   kiddo   we
          all got scars   sweetie   hell
     so you got no feeling in them nipples
     so they're growing back big as ever
                    well   let me tell you   honey
                         knockers bazoogas hooters
               believe me   some would be glad
     if you know what I   in the name of
               the Father   the Son
                         and the Holy
                              Holy

saaaaay but listen   / sister
                    hauled these breasts around the world
                    loaded on a plane loaded on a boat
                         sailing for Thailand
                         looking for an (i)land
               how much land can you stuff in an i
               how many girls western men b(i)
               how much (tow rai)
               too much (peng pai)
               how much (tow rai)
               you've got to be joking (mai kaw chai)

                                                            55

*and that's a pagoda in the photo koh means island no i no land koh
phangan koh samui koh phi phi on inthanon the highest doi mountain
from the village she's a girl her father didn't sell we eat gow pat gai
almost she says he almost sell me to white mans make me slut sweet on
her lips chicken grease sews all day all day money to her father eyes
down brown like what the sun her hands some day some man eyes down
no i no land the sun her fingers chicken grease rice smoke mountain girls
women and*

Kaloka
   Pagoda
      how are you?

✿

Smokes.

In the basement.

When she does the wash before automatics up to her pits in detergent and bleach and bluing and the wringer washer growls.

Old wood 'n coal stove, coal chute, timbers like down the mine and the stench always the stench of sewer gas, some idiot asshole put the cesspool here inside.

Feeds bleachy clothes into wringers with a wooden spoon.

Wipes hands on her pants always stretch fortrel dry in a jiffy jesus you need that in the winter.

Fingers numb from bleach, fingers a handle on the wood 'n coal, her stash, fingers a Player's Plain, jams deep between her fingers.

One two strike the match sweet jesus sulphur and the paper sweet crinkly between her lips.

Sucks, her lips in and in smoke when she was a kid Liver Lips Liver Liver Lips smoke her lungs almost died on the coast Morris More Ass and Tits smoke too friggin damp smoke mother died of asthma heart exploded smoke in lungs in died herself once the coast on her chest slid under her dead mother on top a hill c'mon Evvie you can make it c'mon straddled on her chest an intern bang her heart bang you can make it you can make it

fit, all the its yous shes. not to be clever, clever spaces clever
line-breaks clever rhythms, fuckin'g clever. you in the photo
touched up pink. fierce white frizz, fierce white eyebrows, and
those eyes even then green and glaring. how old, maybe three and
your legs sticking straight out your pink dress. imagine you in a
pink dress and sitting. six kids before you and she was already
dying wasn't she. sucked in cheeks, black under the eyes,
shoulders raised gasping. at night on hands and knees whole body
convulses. you on the steps crying scared shitless when he comes
home pissed raises his fist cracks her cheekbone, don't leave me
you bitch. she holds you close, how else can you say. tight. to her
chest. close. against. her heart bangs ribs shudder. she murmurs
into your sweaty hair. french because that was her mother's
tongue. mother mom mummy ma mère. what language what story
in her head you are she her mother dead asthma heart ruptured
stink of chemical like ether on her breath. her story your story
motherstory. run to the drugstore quickquick hands fisted she
curled into a ball on the bed body quivering. you eleven. scream as
they carry her out on a stretcher, i hate. dark her dead in the night
and you locked outside when they sing.

all herstories. no basement in your trailer. i walk into the
kitchen. you fidget turn your back. i think you've been smoking.
you flee out the door pick up a blanket on the porch hands shake.
flee out into the yard, horses, pasture, and mountains. will not
look back. and Thi running down the hill away. mother crying her
name. boat the crossing mother's hair. mother not. in all the
photos, yes oh yes. not. not here to touch to touch to touch. not.
no. into the bathroom where i am. your head on my shoulder. and
shaking, crying, forty-two years running running from her death,
ran into her this morning, jesus

your mother in the photos.
four-foot-eleven in the photos.
air-starved cheeks
Thi's mom in the
round face
hair pulled back
your mother's hair under a hat
brittle ankles
black around the eyes
like pigeons
in the
in the photos
photos
hair eyes face lips chest hands hips skin
mom. oh mom.

Because Calgary

❖

✿

Leaving Calgary. All your life in this city, how old were you then
26? 27? three kids in the back of the '54 Plymouth, you and Dad
and Dave just a baby between you up front. All of your belongings
our belongings piled in the U-haul behind. Leaving Calgary, and
me hunched in the back seat while the plane streaming 'Happy
Mother's Day,' the plane carrying my friend Tracy Slater and her
mother, the plane I want you to be in so that you can see this city
you were born in, the plane i won us a ride in, but we aren't there
looking down, seeing Calgary all at once, because that's the way
time is. Buzzing. And you there, you here, i can't say tracing,
that's not your word. Walking, smoking, running, skating. And
your mother. Dying. Your father. Drinking. Your sister Edna.
Dying. Yet somewhere in the smells of, tastes of, between beats of
the heart before it stops, maybe even after because time is, you are
skipping, eating chocolate, pounding a home-run out of the park.
But really, it's the physical, your fingers around the bat, terrifying
blood on your underpants after your mother's death, the chemical
smells from her pores, your full lips, me in your seventeen-year
belly, your breasts blue-veins and nipples, and trains shunting
diesel and rust and hot metal on Ninth Ave. s.e., the Cecil and St.
Louis and St. Regis, Kinama Lunch grease and hamburger and
horses and sweat and aspens and the river and home-made
moonshine and lard on home-made bread, all at once, because
time and space, because fingers, lips, and skin.

❁

hands,

    and feet

        all those tongues

and hands

    this city

    talks all night between rivers, Bow and Elbow
        between dams, Bearspaw an imprint on your sleeping
cheek somehow softer in the night , and Glenmore

    talks all night all night

        its hands, this city

    touch a shoulder, sleeping or not
        eyelid   pelvic bone   vertebra back of your
knee, sleeping or not, dying or not

belly

where drunk uncles stagger deserted streets embrace a parking
meter love me love me

where aunts tuck their children all girls all girls and the baby
    into parkas and mitts and scarves
            to the middle of the bridge where the river icy
below lift them over the sides heavy in their

        then jump themselves

    where brothers drive with their wives who came over after
        another woman other children they never see
        full speed into a concrete pillar

where female cousins curl around the breast that is missing
where friends swallow silver or gold because of pain

where

                                        this city
                                        this Calgary
                                        this, here

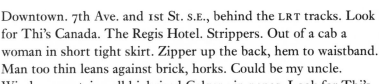

Downtown. 7th Ave. and 1st St. s.e., behind the LRT tracks. Look for Thi's Canada. The Regis Hotel. Strippers. Out of a cab a woman in short tight skirt. Zipper up the back, hem to waistband. Man too thin leans against brick, horks. Could be my uncle. Windows upstairs, all highrised Calgary in panes. Look for Thi's Canada. My grandfather in one of those rooms died drunk.

/they put you up in the Regis
because
you could sleep cheap and so could   /they.
      You couldn't speak English just
a few words you picked up American
not Canadian in the refugee camp six months on
Pulau Bidong.
      /they put you up
in the St. Regis over the bar dressed you in clothes wrapped
two three times around your body thin as rice.
      You walked into the strip joint.   Hey kid hey
girlie wog get get get Christ don't she
(hear)   is where you steal a name comic book so
Cathy

✳

Again on the sidewalk in front of the Regis. Thinking of Thi. And
a man crutches toward me, hey sister could you give me some
money I got in an accident and I got to go home to my reserve but
I got no money for the bus, booze on his breath swaying and I am
caught (four alcoholic uncles on my mother's side), give him the
money (the youngest gave me two hundred dollars once) or say no
(when he drank he shit himself) or call the Friendship Centre to
ask for advice when the man swipes at my face. Cheap bitch.

What did you think when
              they your pyjama
(pyzama you say)   said don't but your sister-in-law
       sewed for you
                    wear in public   take these

wool skirt, fortrel blouse?

❁

Along the Bow River. Walking. Cottonwood, willow, goose shit.
Canada? Christ, how about Calgary, one street even, one
building. The bus barn one block south of the Bow, across from
Eau Claire Lumber office now a restaurant, breakfast all day.
Diesel, oil on cement. Lay in a trench, fiddled in the guts of a bus.
Mother's father. Sober, good friend, good buddy. Piss drunk.
Passed out. Canned. One week later and only a red brick chimney
left. Hole in the ground, and rocks. For a big friggin hotel and
market. Covered so the vegetables don't get rained on.

how long since, Thi
how old when
how much time until

    and her picture her face round like yours

  but so many

      years?
      children?
      plums?
      nights alone alone alone?

        hurry, you said
        I need you, you said
        I wish you were my real mother, you said

Wander around Southeast Calgary. Looking. Fort Calgary flat in the sun a few wooden posts and metallic signs between two rivers. Bow and Elbow. Looking. Rivers a twist a tissue a tongue. Prairie grass and gophers. Man on a bench face away, stands, strikes a match to newspaper, hurls it rolling and flaming in the wind over and over prairie grass. Turns, a brown tweed suit rumpled, eyes sparking blue blue sky. Those eyes. Veers. Hands to the sky blue and sparking. Over prairie grass. Across the street into the alley behind Billingsgate Fish Market.

And how, how about your father, my grandfather?

Bump on the head as a baby?

Rumours of a boxing match when he was a young man and his fist killed

Origins, who knows, Sidney Mines Nova Scotia, Somewhere England, they say different all those aunts and uncles and no help from the Mormons except baptizing for the dead not drunks

Or one cell or group of cells buried in the brain

Alcohol a conductor straight down his arms his fists

Message back a day late too late those purple bruises his children his wife four foot eleven asthmatic and you frizzy blond hair flared nostrils thick lips fierce green eyes hey hit a home run for me little shit that's my

Where his fingers

You waited for him in the dark in beer cigarette stench outside the St. Louis the Regis the Cecil, waited for

Fine man when sober

Jesus, how

Fired from the bus barns worked at Barney's Chicken for Christ
sake finger lickin' good

And at the end on his back upstairs sleezy hotel beer and butts
and fists and dead wife oldest daughter dead dead drunk four
drunk sons

In the hospital won't die until he sees you until he says sorry until

Christ

Bearing Down

about words connections conjunctions
just thinking that's all and not really
clever

But mostly about meat i am thinking
meat but not really
thinking about m-e-e-t, that's what
you and Dad in a greasy spoon, you
serve him lettuce because jockeys can't eat
hamburgers and fries
A man who never changes his baby's diaper says no
no way I'll use cloth and have a pail in my house
shit and water
acid or trees
us however them
yes, but
how many acres for one beef compared with legumes

About Dad's hooked finger, middle digit
Hooking slabs of beef slooooooosh across the block
Hooking how love is a hook
And language, where the conjunctions are because
if i simply thought or said father butcher would be
too easy, and not at all at all what i am thinking but
my baby head crowning
between, and i almost have the connection
between

My brother your son and his wife their baby swimming in plasma
in placenta kicking maybe thinking who knows but my brother
pressing his palms onto the baby drumming drumming inside
waiting to rupture connections my brother pressing his lips
between his hands father brother wife mother sister between
Dad's death my birthday this baby blood between and Thi maybe
seventeen feet in stirrups married three days dead mother father
dead drunk, bearing
bearing down

leave him my father pleads jesus christ can't you see how he looks
at his daughters why are you doing this why are you letting him,
in the dark i am afraid of, always in the dark five years every night
in the dark, rolls over me bald head thick hairy can't breathe arms
pinned can't breathe pushes can't breathe pushes in the dark over
my head chest hard in the dark pushes can't breathe thick hairy
dark pushes, I need you you're my little girl I saw you looking
your brother you fuck him don't you your friends too see how you
hold them you're growing up leaving me I need you I need you I
love you you shouldn't talk to my daughters like that you don't
know about kids I want to give you a baby be my baby I'm worried
about you you want to go out without me I see you looking at all
the guys the women your brother your friends gorgeous gorgeous
keep your hands at your sides keep gorgeous your hands don't
look gorgeous I need don't leave me sssshhhhh don't talk
sssshhhhhh don't talk sssssssssshhhhhhh, push thick hairy can't
breathe my heart spasms womb spasm spasm every cell even my
brain, my fist in the dark his temple in the dark my fist knuckles.
Bone bang bone bang, rolls off me in the dark. And in broad
daylight she marches from their shack, Ev Evelyn Evvie, blood
down her nose two black eyes, marches eyes fierce green, You'll
never touch me again bastard, down the road shimmering, away
away away.

After the dark

        lonely

    basement

talk to me ssssshhhhhh talk to me   sssssshhhhhhhh

          secret from your family

      lonely lonely   Rwuanda

sssssshhhhhhhhhh

        alone to the hospital alone

bury the necklace he

            bury digup bury dig bury   bury

❀

How stories unfold in the brain

In the blood too

> sssssshhhhhh ssssssshhhhh
> ssshhhhh don't tell too
> much who knows who
> might get hurt

Along the nape of the neck, yes
oh yes

> rhymes with Bowness one steel bridge away which uncle
could be
> don't say his name for Christ sake don't say his name

uncle
hotel
yodel

Behind the scab on your knee

> okay blondie little sister little buddie pitch 'er right
> here blondie blondie you can do it eh buddie show
> 'em the stuff show 'em the stuff burn 'er right here
> eh kiddo kiddo

his story too, perched on a bike too big what
maybe eight brush cut white eyebrows in the sun his arm around
you eleven how long after your mother died before your sister
died one year later no one told him where the grave was first drink
at eight your father gave him the bike tipping the photo black and
white and what about his child hand on your shoulder?

Where you begin

Blue veins down your abdomen in a V

Womb like a pear and your voice

> *help me help me somebody help me there's*
> *blood I'm bleeding to death* eleven *god help me*
> *bring her back bring her back*

The pores on her hand before she died

His stomach

what was the story you told his story born without a
lining in his stomach the only one younger than you
starving to death his belly blown up air and her fingers
rub and drum and stroke until he is old enough for ether
and a sheep lining

In the tip of your tongue tasting your palette, the hard one

the question is how you didn't drink or your
sisters or your oldest brother and all the deaths
the longing the shame the handsome brothers
that feeling in the brain the groin all the years
his first drink at eight for Christ's sake run
out of town at sixteen knife on his hip and
how the words in your green eyes and his and
his daughters' tawny hair and eyes like cats
who won't see him will never see him and the
question all those years is what

Even the flesh between your fingers

it's the bike

tipping

the tongue

tipping

the   bottle

and those fumes

heat behind the eyes

and the longing

,how do you write

longing

✿

I didn't blame myself, she says, I blamed Shirley Temple. He
grabbed me downtown, dragged me out past the tracks, kept
saying what he'd like to do to little girls like Shirley Temple. Bit
me all over, went to get a rock to finish me off. Shirley Temple, I
thought, goddamn you Shirley Temple. Couldn't swim, but
crossed the river. Blood ran down my legs, knocked on three doors
no one came. Then an old lady opened her door, Oh darling,
hugged and hugged me blood all over, called the police. Sat in the
back with a police woman, wrapped me in a blanket held onto me.
Got my mom from her sick bed her dying bed, died three months
later. Thought I killed her.

& what if
you had left your brother's home basement your other brother's
    apartment Helen your nieces nephew Vietnamese lemon grass
    pyjama your sister-in-law sewed all the smells the sounds music
    & more
        beside the river green
        beside the river, seagulls, an osprey, cottonwood
        beside, each other on limestone boulders, breathing
        each & other & the river green & a pineapple bun a
            black bean rice cake & the river, breathing breathing,
            especially, green
        the words 'be' & 'side', fingers ribs heart spleen &
            memories in our cells, twenty-four days with her
            eleven years fifteen children three still with her
            tired strong you will not ask her for will not, the
            weight of mmmmmm other
    or lost child

                        river & breathe & be &
                        green &
                            if?

if you were my real mother,

who would my father be?

in the Philippines, and how many years since

your face like hers

and how

your longing

Thi

✾

all in the shape of

                              how her nostrils flare and her lips
          thick years of teasing only now they use silicon
                  and her round arms, legs, shoulders cocked in the sun
                          bird maybe
          bat back then pivot, swing, one motion every cell

                  and Thi, long fingers arching between joints
                          long feet waist hair long
          round face but not really
                                  more in her eyes and lips reading silence
          and her hair curtains her shoulders too big she says for
          Vietnamese
                          and the mango   red bean cake   ginseng tea
                  stuff in my pack,   her long long arms

                                          babies' heads

          the light round glaring when i go under
          the nurses' hands light along my arm
          and the doctor's as she leans over
          and light fizzles up my arms explodes every cell with white light
          in the back of my throat and the soft nerves in my eyes the
          light i don't see penetrate my abdomen
          illuminate seven black flecks like pepper
          illuminate the swelling and nausea and cramps
          illuminate angels on the head of fibre optics
          and the antiseptic toilet with blood
          illuminate the uterus' emptiness, except for blood

the trout on the grill
the trout over the open fire
the trout with its head back
roasting on the grill over the open fire

the grandmother's breasts in a hotel room in Revelstoke B.C.
the way pines fan out at the bottom and mountains
the way she sat on the edge of the bed
  lifted her arms while trees burned and red curtains and carpets
  lifted her arms over her head
the way smoke filled the valley
the valleys in Wales years and years ago
the way her arms, her young arms, circled the baby in her
  christening gown
the way she knew everybody in the valley in Wales
the boat that carried them across the ocean
the train to Saskatchewan
the gullies and prairie and bluffs and three young children and
  horses and space and sky and her husband underground and
  flatness and sky pressing, pressing
    lifted her blouse and slip over her head
    lifted her pink nightgown over her head

the word love
lemon
lobelia
labia

stolen books in a pink shoulder bag

in a cloth pink shoulder bag

edges and corners of stolen books

digging into the pink shoulder

on the street, on the bus, the LRT

edges and corners and frames of stolen books and paintings and
prints her shoulders her hip

joints and corners and edges stolen books art books nature books
prints paintings hardcover novels up the stairs through the door
into the illegal apartment

stolen books pink bag shoulder cloth edges frames paintings
corners walls doors books prints walls frames illegal corners edges
apartment frames books illegal corners walls alone illegal

shoulder shoulder shoulder

six tiny tea cups and a tiny tea pot on a tray
from China Town and the pot she
gave, the whispered phone calls
how after gives the impression of order of linearity
except the cups and pot round like the tray
and our heads small, bodies round
an Oriental perspective Weyman Chan says given our
round faces small bodies its all a matter of perspective
whose eyes whose body whose mouth whose

sip

being eleven when your mother dies in
the night and you never see
being eleven when your mother stands on
the shore calling your name but you can't
being eleven when you are twelve and
your sister dies your father smashes you kick and bite but
being eleven when you are thirteen and
one of your sisters writes tells you your sister the gentle one
died because
being eleven when you are seventeen and
between your thighs your baby's head
being eleven when you are seventeen and
alone and anaesthetic like garlic
being eleven when you are fifty-three your
daughter grieving her empty womb walks into your kitchen your
mother mummy ma mère
being eleven when you are twenty one or
two or three and at last your mother travels from Vietnam to
the Philippines to San Jose phones and says she has cancer
somewhere reproductive
being eleven and being told to look, look
after   look out   look

that pear long-necked or mango or fist, depending on whose or
when

      how we move around it all our organs moving
    even our pelvic bones scooped and flying
    even when it's removed full of cysts or cancer
    even when radioactive dyes sit in our cervix
    even when we bleed or don't with the moon

because this soft
because   this muscular
    this pear mango or fist

    and this is where we started

    the word mother in so many languages
    begins with the lips together

Between Beats

Enis Petrini drives because my mom doesn't, my dad says Why do
you want to drive anyway I don't want my wife driving, except
down to our horse pasture when he's at work and once through
the Frank Slide, stopped by the cops, You're going too slow, lady,
dangerous as speeding. Enis Petrini behind the wheel i can't
breathe shoulders to ears can't breathe trapped can't breathe
trapped chest tight muscles tight push tight push tight pull tight
on my hands tight knees tight help tight chest help tight help
shiver help tight help. Enis drives our '63 Pontiac through the
Frank Slide through Blairmore, trees houses rock my body
trapped quivers, to the hospital outside Blairmore, boulders coal
my chest, Help me mom i hurt, carries me into a room white light
and my chest shoulders heart quivers, slides the needle into my
arm my vein the doctor nurse my mom, Bang my heart, puke up
my throat on the nurse, heart beat beat beating and air oh air in in
in out out out. In the hospital bed, half sitting, alone because she
has to hitch-hike because he just doesn't, plastic mouthpiece suck
in air and chemical wet the back of my throat my lungs, hold, my
stomach turns, it's okay it's okay, hold hold, out, my stomach the
sun above my bed, alone. Tuesday, Wednesday, Thursday, Friday,
Saturday, they bring her in on Sunday, tiny wet shivering black
under her eyes, shoulders to ears wheezing chest fluttering eyelids
fluttering, drop her off and leave. They beat her, the nurses
whisper, look at these bruises, put her in a crib in the next room.
All day i stand beside her crib watch her chest quiver pale skin
black eyes all evening. Opens her eyes, stares up at me. Carrie? i
say, Carrie Carrie. Stands up reaches for me. All night hold her in
my bed. Smiles at me, touches my face, sleeps her head warm
sweaty against my ribs. All day, two, three, play with her feed her
she laughs out loud holds her arms up around my neck holds on,
her heart, my heart, thin skin thin ribs thin membranes. Cries
when they pick her up, stands looking out the pick-up window so
small so pale, the woman thin blonde hair the man long black
light a smoke drive off saying who knows what and inside standing
on my bed looking out, my heart my heart.

and Evvie, between you and Thi in a movie
between you and Thi over coffee, Thi laughing and talking,
letting herself

you and Thi and always your mothers always
their hands and
voices and the warm pocket of
skin of air of what under their chins
between the muscle holding the shoulder and the heart,
always that

and how soft with blue veins the temple and the heart contracts
fibrillates flutters, all the memories of
and Thi asks you if you considered abortion
when you were seventeen and pregnant and you say no, but

❖

Edna in the photo.

Edna sounds like Edward, a name your father's, Ed na, in a
bathing suit leaning into a Cottonwood, one knee slightly raised.

A woman's face in the shape of her kneecap.

The sun shines in her eyes, Edna Edna, her eyes without their
round wire-frame glasses, because she has been swimming in the
Elbow River.

Because, a photo.

Because black and white and death.

Because Edna, when you say her name Edna, say your sister and
the love in your voice.

The love in your voice, sun, and.

She squints, leans the soft insides of her arms, leans her wet
swimsuit with the skirt and her puckered nipples and her cheek,
the cheek her mother your mother rubs wet diapers on because it
is good for the skin, into warm wood.

Because all the photos, our tongues between our teeth, and
breath.

Yes, the smells of, and sleeping in the same bed,
the way the body makes a warm moist pocket of, the way the
body does that.

You and Edna under the quilt upstairs,
the smell of your mother's heart,
the smell of the cells' electricity before the heart explodes,
smell of breath unbreathed.
The way the body
remembers.

You and Edna under the quilt, she is
smelling the wind and the grass in your hair, she is
smelling the salt in your tears, she is
smelling the hardness of
the back of your head your eleven-year-old head in the pocket
between her arm and breast, death in the present tense, and even
the vowels smell.

If there were oranges, she would smell them.

Her body would. Rolling in bed, raising an arm,
furling leg over leg over leg,
that moisture, scent,
its very own.

How did he smell when you walked through the long yellow grass beside the river in the sun your mother in bed not breathing dying on her hands and knees on her back dying her cells screaming screaming, how when he attacked you from behind his breath and fingers and who knows what he ate for lunch who he kissed, running, how does it smell blood, fear, and where in you in your cells the nerves behind your eyes your green eyes does this stench live?

Your father, too, alcohol on his breath, but that was after

You and Edna under the quilt. The very
insistence of. Eleven and twenty. And she smells like
your mother. Present tense.

The way the body remembers. Loving Edna because she is your
sister smells like river like talc like milk like mother like skating on
the outdoor ice. Blood too, meningitis, how does it smell in her
brain, twenty-one, and urine as every cell lets go as Edna lets go as
electricity leaks out of every cell in the bed you share and the
doctor on the phone says two aspirins can you pay? how?

Thi, too, and Helen on the fourteenth floor in the apartment
  the mother's photo on the shelf, the brother out cleaning
offices at night, huddled not the right word, in the same bed
  trying to talk but Thi dreaming her mother in Vietnam
dreaming rice through her fingers the river slow and warm the
  colour green and her teacher her Canadian teacher her friend
here in the apartment meat boiling in a big pot on the stove
  reading Thi's mother in Vietnam listening in the apartment,
Vietnamese singing, Helen's back turned to her in the
  dark dreaming herself graduating the school of technology on
the hill a traditional marriage a job in an oil company and her
  reading dreaming silent sister Thi and smells, smells from the
body, while on the street leaves turn yellow turn sweet.

More a question of.

What smells do you remember, Kaloka, Pagoda
        upstairs in gramma's old bed my back to you, draw a
        picture on my bare skin, guess house, guess tree,
        giraffe, Turtle Mountain, and the wind shakes,
        shakes, the window panes.

Especially the way your nose twitches
the way you smell the fingerprints on pens, lip-prints in the
spoon's hollow, sworls and space between
your fingernails and skin.

Where in the cells memories of smell lie dormant
, how,
and how they taste.

In the desert in Northern China when the police wake you up in
the middle of the night in the bed where you are sleeping, where
your arms and thighs and your stomach already feeling sick, haul
you outside put you on a bus, or in Pakistan blood in your stool
vomit in the back of your throat the intravenous sliding in, what
smells what memories what sister?

Or

shivering in the middle of the bed, your
fingertip tracing my skin, the warm space between
my flannelet pyjama my back and your hand, and the cold
cold smell of dirt on the windowsill.

fear?

And the other sister, Muriel, at the train station,
grief over Edna over her mom locked in her hand,
at the train station, diesel in her lungs and the aneurysm
will kill her smell her taste her at fifty-one,
nineteen years after her daughter
dies on the operating table
the electricity in her heart
short-circuit in her heart
with a hole, just like,
at the train station, what, fourteen fifteen waiting for the train,
    looking west looking west looking west?

Except when you stay with her in Banff.
Except when you work in the hospital with her in Banff
it's her hair, the smells, it's her hair dark hair growing out
of follicles in her scalp, follicles in her scalp
covering her skull, grey matter,
and the vein with soft walls, the vein with a soft bulge,
where smells,
carbolic soap, pine, blood, urine, ether,
especially ether.

You and Edna under the quilt. The way the body remembers.

You and your mother under the quilt, and the way the body

You and a friend at her house and during the night all the electricity in her cells the warm moist pockets, memories and urine leak out, leak into her bed where, you, hug, her, cold

Two of your children upstairs in the house in Bellevue on their hands and knees their sweaty blue-veined bodies jerk convulse shudder

You and dad in the dark side-by-side in the grimy motel in Calgary because he won't stay in anyone else's home while the chemicals leak out his pores, or at home in Bellevue weeks and weeks while the chemicals leak out his pores, morphine leaks out his pores, and his memories your memories, his eyes running wide-open in the dark, willing his body, but it won't, and your body beside him numb on the bed while in the space below the ceiling you

With your lover on the ranch, mountains outside and horses, the warm moist pockets between you, chewing tobacco, Youth Dew, oats, whisky on his breath, liver spots on his skin, age on his skin, cells sloughing off and the air sacs in his lungs swell his tissues swell air in his connective tissues carbon dioxide in his lungs sitting up in bed trying to cough trying to breathe out trying to breathe, while your mother

the time your father on a drunken dare staggered the cemetery
over by the Stampede ground where maybe your dead mother
stabbed a grave, caught his cuff, lay pinned
all night, thinking a dead hand

            the time you wanted to kiss the boy

called you More Ass and Tits ran his bike
        into the Elbow River down by the horse barns,
                    put him in a head-
lock,
            dunked his whole head and body,
            kissed him on the mouth when he came up for

when we lived in Bridgeland over by the General Hospital,
        the tiny houses with big gardens,
            with gardens full of carrots and kohlrabi and spinach
and onions,
        all our Italian neighbours,
                    you brought
Kaloka

when your baby brother stopped drinking when Anne moved into
the trailer with him in Sparwood B.C. cleaned up the shit the
bottles the puke because he needs a mother his mother dead when
he was eight and you can see he never grew up, mothered him
then left, he don't need me no more I done my job now I got my
grandkids things to do, he joined A.A. on the wagon not the same
as a dry drunk it's the thinking that's different, living on the edge
of the Hutterite colony with a woman from there and her
daughter with the hole in her heart,

phoned and said he loved

hefting huge blocks of cheese after
                        dad died died died

     as if verbs as if lingual as if
          his tongue hands eyes hips singing
singing singing singing   as if

                    choice

     hoisting and wrapping cheese in the steaming Bellevue dairy
          milk and hot plastic and
                    salt, clean fine salt,
leaks out

what were you seeing, dad beside you eyes open wide on his back
in bed while the curtains fluttered while his heart the skin over
white and thin fluttered his liver bulging with cancer cells
explode in the back of his brain?

the missing spleen
the spleen cut away and the neat scar
the spleen cut away, the neat scar, and the hole
the hole inside, in the dark, under the smallest curved
rib, fibrillating

on the bed, because prepositions
because position, the mattress smooth or lumpy
sheets or not, wind and sweat

or in the mud, gunpowder or mustard gas or radiation on the
wind, say, or kneeling gagged over the bathtub each blow
punctures her skull and the man behind her and her friend tied
on the bed downstairs hearing and the nurses after she is dead
asking him on the forensic, unit they say, why or what did you
feel, or numbers, how a woman is raped every 17 minutes in
Canada, every 3 in the u.s., how 50,000 people die under buildings
because the earth, we say, contains faults

water, memory

memory of trihalomethanes and trichloroethylene
of zinc, lead, cadmium, dioxins, furans
aluminum in water, in the brain cells losing
memory, scrambling fibres of

the deer beside the river stretching her neck breaking the
surface tension of
her nose black
and soft, or the fish, the rainbow trout or sockeye salmon or
arctic char

remember that finny fibrillation?

remembers the Bow River how it starts

a stream a fall   over rocks, black

   from a glacier   centuries of ice

centuries and centuries of water flowing out of rocks under the
earth out of glaciers all the streams and rivers flowing through
limestone through sandstone through coulees and valleys through
mountains picking up picking up picking up

water in all our cells
water remembering us

, how breath speaks for cells down deep dark, the body
remembers, and the heart we say

, oh the heart

Moon Sea She

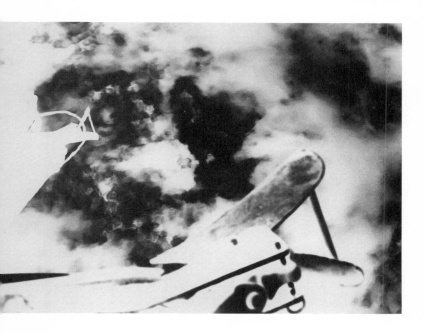

✣

how
how all these poems want to begin with
and Thi means poetry in Vietnamese
how lines insist insist repeat repeat
and you cannot see no you cannot see much into the sea
bulbous weeds and snaky, those rubbery fronds fingers reaching
how phosphorescence around the boat or oars when you pee or
spit or row

sparks is the word, the verb under the surface
friends and frauds and sparks in the hold
if you have one, or the act of holding
in my arms, your arms, her arms
how the anchor if you have one holds or doesn't
messages from weeds or mud or sand or rock on the bottom
not the bodies hopefully not the cousin laughing in the village
starving on the boat rolled over the side
up fifty feet of chain and rode to your hands
holding
or not

how you never see your own cervix
or feel your boat swing in the night change your sense of place
of order of perception of
try the verb, touches, how my cousin touches the tumour eating
darkness inside her breast
or hold, how Thi's cousin holds the man's hand who is her
husband tonight who is sixteen years older who was a teacher in
Vietnam who is

holds herself stiff, all the women who are afraid
walking alone down the dark street past dark doors
waiting for the rent cheque not to bounce
hands on their babies' foreheads in the night
hands on their own vulva in the night
afraid of the leeches from swimming in mud
afraid of the leeches crawling up inside

the word is merciless
mercy and merci being cousins

how the tide can flow one way the current another the wind
another and the boat up a wave and i am weightless hanging,
hanging on and Thi at the cousin's wedding just back from her
mother in San Jose ten years of longing her mother's cancer
cervical not ovarian a blue-white buddha around her neck and
Helen's from their cousin an arranged marriage knew him two
months the older sisters and brothers why are you so late Thi has
been waiting and the chopsticks mushrooms spicy fish and the
younger brother and sisters four months from Vietnam the oldest
brother's band his voice the latin rhythms all the cousins and
aunts and uncles and in-laws and friends and Thi's hair cut short
cut elegant her long traditional tunic the singing laughing talking
in Vietnamese all the boats in the harbour all the boats at sea all
the boats becalmed pirates boarding all the boats leans over says
she misses her mother already says her mother is modern says she
wants to move there right away on the green chair in the living
room in the dark says all this guilt this shame they don't know me
i can't tell my mother she will feel sorry for afraid i will lose you
afraid i will lose the you inside all the brothers and sisters
different except for maybe the eyebrows the cha-cha rhumba
tango

the smell of boats, especially at sea

smell of naming :

        ropes

        oil

        diesel

        sweat

        canvas

        seaweed

        bilge

        shit

        methane

        clams

not to mention, because words are merciless

not to mention women with our hands between our legs

some of us not afraid of leeches

unafraid of the smell of boats

how the man on his boat his home tells the woman to change the
water in the clam pail

how to dump the water in the bilge drop the bucket over the
side for more

how to work the diesel stove and the little hanging one boiling
clams

how to put up the jib and mainsail

how to walk ondeck

how to tie herself to a lifeline in a stiff wind

how a man overboard is

how no one says 'woman'

how no one says 'she'

except, the boat

except, the sea

where pronouns lie seals swim eyes open pups otters
sea-weed fern-weed frond-weed ripples salt moon
                                                    and the tide

while the men onboard the boat talk about boats

while the men onboard talk about where they've been

while the men onboard talk

when we name ourselves hands on our vulva sweat salt and
sweet stinging oh the moon the moon tide on the flow on the
moon mons soon heat under sweat under   slide slide
thighs water up to cool and the salt floating flowing
name hum moon sea she vulva and sweet oh sweet sweat salt
monsoon mom move move moon   she she   me   mer et mère
name ourselves we hands our vulva sweat salt and sweet
stinging

                    the moon

            naming

  sweet

                        ourselves

        sting wording my

                she

    the word the word

                vulv   aaaaaa

            ma   ma   mère

                    more

        my and we

                beeeeee youuuuuuuuuu thiiiiiiii

✳

how the doctor where she worked walked the green length of
corridor eyes on her breasts not once looking away

how one morning she fixed her eyes on his crotch way at the
other end marched the whole length green green her vision
and his crotch

how she waitressed at the Stampede Bar and Grill maybe sixteen
joked with the jockeys walked Christmas eve in the snow with
asked him to sing and sing

how she grew up in Calgary white trash

how she left Vietnam without her mom

how she grew up in the Crowsnest

how her sister died in Vietnam poisoned fetus in her womb

how her brother-in-law   and she couldn't tell

how her sister in a Calgary shack slipped into a coma   aspirin
the doctor said   too late too poor dead in two days

how her sister in the Crowsnest

how her sisters

how she lost her mother when she was eleven

how she stood outside the funeral home while they sang

how her mother's hair brushes Vietnamese soil

how her mother in the Crowsnest pitches baseball

how her mother in Vietnam feeds the pigs harvests plums
draws water trudges to market while her father in the city
with his mistress

how her mother runs twelve machines at Phillips Cables a man's
job shift work while her father the singer with his

how she met him in the library because she refuses to eat reads
and reads English takes it in her pores and he is black and
lonely

how she slips all hours into his basement apartment can never be
seen together Vietnamese and Rwuandan groin aching
combined loneliness

how she was raped the year her mother died a park in Calgary
worked at twelve ran from the police a week in jail and the
jockey sang to her in her room

how men and boys assume she is a slut because her breasts

how frying hamburgers and chips made her vomit for five months
no not flu the doctor said and she told the jockey as he was
boarding a box car for Seattle with horses

how she was underage and bribed her molesting brother-in-law to
sign the consent form

how she married the jockey three days before the baby

how she went alone to the hospital thought she would die before
and after and the man from Rwuanda never

how 23 women came back from Hawaii pregnant leaky condoms
and she was

how every month her womb empties itself

how her friend told her hand on her abdomen about the baby
combined loneliness and the plans for an abortion, downtown in
a jungle and she couldn't say

how people pat her on the back don't try so hard

how she couldn't say she would love to adopt and her friend had
to go alone to the hospital

how her sister never heard from the man in Hawaii

how her arms ache

how she might have been that baby

how she grieved over possible people grieved over women's
grief

how she avoids the first person pronoun

how her friend said she wanted to crawl inside her and be

how

how she

Thanks to:

Fred Wah, Jane Warren, Ashok Mathur, and Nicole Markotic for your support, encouragement, and expertise.

The women from *Truck, an artist run centre* for sharing your images with me.

Stan Dragland & Marnie Parsons for your sensitive readings.

Roberta Rees was born in New Westminster, B.C. She was raised in the village of Bellevue in the Crowsnest Pass, and now lives in Calgary where she has taught high school and university English courses and now teaches Creative Writing for Women. Her work has appeared in such journals as *The New Quarterly, Event, blue buffalo, Fireweed* and *Prism International* and in several chapbooks. *Eyes Like Pigeons* is her first book.